Cover Art:
Johannes Vermeer
The Art of Painting, circa 1666
Oil on Canvass
Kunsthistorisches Museum,
Wien oder KHM
Wien

The

PSYCHOLOGICAL   ELEGANCE

of

TALENT

The

PSYCHOLOGICAL   ELEGANCE

of

TALENT

by

PHILLIP HATHAWAY

Hardcastle Publishing
New York

ISBN-13:   978-0-9796844-3-2

"Come my friends. 'Tis not
too late to discover a new world."

Lord Tennyson

to

GUINEVERE

Table of Contents

Author's Foreword

Imagine yourself when a child of six. Typically, you would have been attending the first grade.

All the newness was frightening and may have caused a feeling like roller-coaster-stomach. At other times, you were thrilled by the idea of spending time with people like yourself, yet sometimes overwhelmed by a kaleidoscopic array of unbridled ecstasy exploding in mingled profusion throughout your "brave new world." Those were the triumphant moments when you laughed and laughed.

Now, suppose you must remain indoors. Suppose you were forbidden to play with the other children for the whole school year. You were forced to read books you didn't like or understand and write sentences miserably slow because they were as alien to you as the arithmetic problems you rarely solved. All the while you listened to the ever increasing squeals and peels upon peels of laughter in multi-tiered rounds from your classmates reveling in recess. Silently staring at your cold lunch, their delighted laughter, virgin romances, five minute battles, courage, bravery, broken hearts and athletic miracles were exacting cruelty. This caused unavoidable tears which you knew the others would see and condemn your situation further by creating the perfect target for their scornful laughter. Yet your teacher, who sentenced you to this imppiteous solitaire for the entire first grade, watched heartlessly, satisfied only with the knowledge that you could not do the very thing for which you longed the most—*to play.*

Now imagine that, although completely innocent, you *asked* to be punished in this way. In fact, you insisted upon it although what you desired most deeply was to play.

Of course, that's preposterous. Why would you ask to be kept indoors and punished as others played while you yourself were longing to join them? No one would do that, would they?

Yes, many people live this way because they have missed their calling and have, they presume, wondered too far away to find it again. But it is never, never too late to use our talent. It is true, to miss one's calling is to be led away from the threshold of abundance to a wilderness, long in monotonous searching. Yet, there remains a path of triumphant return. This book may be a welcomed traveling companion along that bright path.

Should you have already discovered your talent and developed it to the very pinnacle, make this book your friend for it will yet strengthen your virtuosities.

This book will especially help young adults flourish like strong healthy vines in the richest soil—their idiopathic talent. For, the elegant effect of talent upon the mind is a phenomenon of splendor, of limitless grandeur and of common, everyday practicality.

You see, one of the more practical things we can do in life is to parlay our life-episodes into dynamic talent. This is the thing, perhaps the only thing, that perennially redeems us unto our original selves, *for it allows us to play.*

The Unfulfilled Wish

PROCRASTINATION IS REHEARSAL for death! The words flashed cross my mind as I walked into an artist's studio in which it was apparent he had not been honest about his work. This lack of completeness, this lack of truthfulness manifested itself in dozens of his paintings which exhibited *bona fide* talent less the first obligation of artistry: the depth, the lyrical interpretation of sorrow and joy, the artist's idiopathic translation of life. He was not releasing himself to abandonment, the purest act of truthfulness. An unsettling feeling, the thought I may be guilty of the same offense, lodged itself in my stomach.

I beheld a mirror.

I was guilty of not standing unguarded before my audience. I was not letting go somehow. Why was reluctance attached to my deepest wish to perform?

We shall answer that question by looking at the irreducible roots of the problem which are closely associated with the unfulfilled wish. But first we must understand the nature of the conscious mind and, particularly, the subconscious mind where the unfulfilled wish resides. Only then will we be able to understand the satisfaction of the unfulfilled wish and, in so doing, understand *the psychological elegance of talent.*

The Conscious and Subconscious Mind

Now, to begin, let's consider this simple but important story:

Once upon a fleeting moment—yes, all in a fleeting moment sparkling so brightly—in a quaint little village, there lived two shopkeepers named Jack and Jane who owned a very lovely widget shop. Appropriately, they called it *Jack and Jane's Widget Shop.*

One day Jane went on vacation for a month and in her absence big Jack threw a lusty party. Afterwards, he decided he would run their widget shop just the way he wanted. No longer would he be constrained by the myriad of Jane's limits. Now he would expand their tiny operation by selling more than widgets; they would begin to sell beautiful paintings and sculptures. His imagination accelerated as he began to dream of becoming the greatest shop in all the world; they would expand to each and every continent. His dreams were boundless. In fact, now that Jane was gone, he possessed no concept of impossibility. He began to imagine selling everything—literally everything! He told a friend about his grandiose ambitions who suggested a marketing plan but Jack nixed that idea and roared, *"Who needs plans?"*

As Jack dreamt of unparalleled success, customers were complaining that they could not get widgets. They waited outside the shop for the doors to open but Jack was at home mesmerized by his own adventurous plans yet doing nothing practical about them; he didn't even go the shop to open it for the morning's business.

He finally came to the shop at midday, unshaven and sloppily dressed and when a customer asked about purchasing a widget, Jack rambled on incoherently about selling bicycles in Istanbul. The shop was an unkept wreck and the customers stopped coming for widgets.

When Jane returned from vacation she was shocked at the discombobulated condition of the shop and said, "Jack, let's see the books."

"I've decided not to do books anymore! We're going to be the greatest shop in all the world!" Jack's eyes were wild with the lust of ambition. Firmly able-bodied and wieldy Jack had not yet learnt that he was, apart from Jane, a wild man whose limitless will was without boundaries, unable to step aside from the

fiercest confrontation.

While gently touching Jack's arm and with a tender voice, the only voice to which he would truly listen, Jane said, "Let's sit down, Jack. Now, let's get things in order."

They looked at the books and discovered that not a single widget had been sold since she left for vacation. She proceeded to tell him why they could never be the biggest and best shop in the world and why they should continue to sell just a few widgets each day. With Jane's logical assessment of why his plans could never work, she convinced him to commence business as usual. "Jack, just think of all the limits which the world imposes upon us."

Simultaneously shoving his hands deep into his trouser pockets while cocking his head to the side and glancing at the floor with the whimsical smile of an embarrassed child repenting of a naughtiness, he answered, "You're right, Jane." His rough, burley voice betrayed his boyish demeanor and he met her eyes with a broad grin. "Within your logic is sterling wisdom . . . it's always that way with you. Thank you, my dear.

"Jane, now that you're back from vacation, maybe I should take some time off and rest. What'd think?"

With Jane's blessing, unaware that this meant trouble for them both, she bid farewell to Jack and he left for a holiday.

Jane breathed a sigh of relief, then dove into the books and in a few hours balanced them perfectly. Then she cleaned the shop perfectly. Next, every widget was cleaned and placed in just the right position—all alike—perfectly. Several customers came by but she was far too busy organizing and cleaning to attend to their needs or to sell them a widget. The remainder of the day she worried. She worried about taxes, rent, her health, Jack's health, the widget market, competition, the past, the present, the future. Soon, she over-whelmed herself with thoughts of the things which were impossible. In fact, she couldn't think of a single thing that *was* possible. So she gave up. She began closing down the shop and a feeling of hopelessness bore down upon her as a heavy anchor which would drag her to the depths of despondency.

She felt old.

Then upon returning from vacation, Jack walked in

and, noticing her sad deposition, was instantly troubled himself and with tears said, "My precious Jane! What's wrong?"

"I don't know Jack. For some reason we didn't sell a single widget the whole time you were gone. Nothing seemed possible and I gave up. But now that you're back, I know we can sell widgets just like before."

These intimate conversations about their true feelings were healthy and, much, much more, they were necessary. Jane openly admitted that Jack was, by far, the stronger partner. After all, it was he who dreamt up the idea of starting the shop. But she candidly stated, without uncertainties, that she didn't like the way Jack went about things and, likewise, Jack laughed and said, *"Jane, you drive me crazy, too!"* They both laughed, entertaining themselves with openhearted levity about the other's idiopathic quirks 'til tears came to their eyes.

Then Jane, who stood on her tiptoes before brawny Jack, threw her arms round his neck awakening a reminiscence of her dearest childhood feelings that, before this moment, she had buried beneath the dreariness of calculated process and a thousand monotonous details. A magical feeling attuned to Sun-kissed dew drops on the pedals of virgin wild flowers spread across an undiscovered alpine meadow was released from her previously chained up heart and radiated from her countenance in transcendent glow. Then with rough-hewn hands Jack gingerly brushed back a lock of Jane's flaxen hair from her exquisite face and they were almost startled by the presence of light in each other's eyes as one seldom sees. And, for only a moment, they stopped breathing, then looking away, smiled as though they had stumbled upon a secret.

Their undisguised feelings had an endearing effect to the heart and they grew to care for one another more deeply, realizing how very much they needed each other. And, because they instinctively knew that a principle act of love is listening, they began quietly listening to the other and, in turn, to hear each other more clearly, empathically seeing each other in an entirely new light which caused a gentle but powerful magnetism between them.

Never before had they truly noticed and appreciated the sublime subtleties of the other which now appeared powerfully attractive. They both thought to themselves, "How could I have missed it before?" And they became deliberately sensitive to the other, not wanting to miss anything in the future.

Jack and Jane's Widget Shop was back to normal but now normality was so much better than before. They learned that overt optimism could be as dangerous as overt pessimism. They were reconciled with the fact that they were more than coworkers; they needed each other. With Jack's creativity, enthusiasm and enormous drive balanced with Jane's expert accounting and realistic approach to marketing, they steadily expanded the business and, over time, richly prospered. Jack and Jane realized that together they compensated for their mutual deficiencies, excelling while in the other's presence. Indeed, they couldn't live without each other. They continued to deeply value the other's feelings by patiently, sensitively listening to each other.

That value became a lasting love. After their brilliantly white wedding and first night together, they arose early and visited a garden . . .

Tremulous with the presage of dawn, the leaves gently rustled as though stirred from sleep to rejoice, once again, as a member of the peaceable kingdom of hyacinths, morning songsters, brooks pathed through barely fields, heather, forests and a wealth of livingness within them. In spontaneous union, Jack and Jane stood stock still for a moment upon the threshold of this living temple as though they were about to step into a sanctuary where they had no right to enter. Awed by this natural palace to which Jack had welcomed her and the things which, to her, were before invisible, Jane, slowly at first, began to reverently explore its manifold wonders—its inexhaustible wonders and finally to luxuriate in them. This newfound world, the world of her heritage of which she was previously unaware, was the answer to the Eternal question which continually posed itself within her mind, vouchsafed by Jack's presence.

Several weeks later, Jane's friend, Jennifer, popped in unexpectedly for tea and was instantly taken aback by Jane's new look of serene self-assurance radiating from her face.

"You look so rested," said Jennifer. "You've been eating healthy food, exercising and sleeping very soundly, haven't you?"

Surprised, Jane said, "Not any more than I always do. Nothing's changed. Everything's as usual."

"But you look ten years younger, don't you?"

"Oh, thank you," said Jane. "I don't know . . ." Jane was glowing. "I suppose it's Jack. I know its sounds funny but Jack makes me feel so young and beautiful—so clean and fresh—Jack makes me feel that way."

"I don't mean to be quizy but . . . "

"No, not at all. You see, as long as I'm completely honest and truthful in every way—not just with Jack but with everyone—Jack will do anything and everything for me. I need only ask. Jack is so sweet and faithfully loving to me. His strength is unfathomable, it seems, and he guards me by sending feelings, in a sort of telepathic way, so I know the right thing to do."

"Do continue," Jennifer urged with a tone of astonishment.

"Just yesterday, I met a horribly frightful man and I could feel, right in the pit of my stomach, Jack sending a message, *'Jane, avoid this person. He's not well and refuses all help!'*

"As long as we listen to one another, we are so, so much happier together than when alone. I've experienced a heightened sense of awareness of which

I was previously unaware. I see myself as others do, to an extent, and this has caused me to apologize to Mr. Pickering. After all these years I can see his position and how I was selfish in the matter. But now it's over and we're better friends than before. I never thought that would've been possible. Not only that, Jennifer, now I see an entire world which was previously invisible to me. You know, I never noticed the lovely irises, tulips and lilies which surround your cottage. And, oh! The blue bonnets!"

"Oh, Jane! We've planted them every Spring since I was a child!"

Jennifer was, at once, perplexed, fascinated and drawn to Jane's serene energy and abundance.

"Yes," said Jane, now with majestic calmness. "I've seen the blue bonnets every year. But now I'm fully aware of them for the first time—saturated in blue and fragrant.

"Yet, it's not just the flowers. I'm aware of so many good things which were previously invisible to me. All things have become new for us. Jack and I have discovered a life of simplicity, austerity and lucidity. Simplicity, austerity and lucidity allow us to . . . I don't know . . . I suppose it allows us to *not* miss life."

Jennifer and Jane stepped out of time, as it were, and relaxed in rich conversing and the comfort of their old and, now, new friendship.

The marriage of Jane Conscious and Jack Subconscious is the union we wish to emulate. As you may have guessed, the widget shop and Jack and Jane's marriage is representational of our life and, more specifically, our mind. In this story the cerebral mechanics of optimal productivity were fine-tuned achieving what I call *psychosynthesis*—that sublime equilibrium of the conscious and subconscious mind.

From the moment we are born to our last breath, every thought, every word, every action is an attempt to marry the conscious and subconscious; all living things seek to be whole and the balance of the mind is this wholeness which mankind seeks; those of us who find this balance are those who experience the most fulfillment.

Of course, it's not easy. That's why Carl Jung said, "Seldom or never does a marriage develop into an individual relationship smoothly and without crisis.

There is no birth of consciousness without pain."

But the marriage of Jack and Jane had an advantage because it was predicated upon this very important fact: Jack was much stronger than Jane. In other words, Jack subconscious will always have his way. Jane realized this. But because Jack loved her with fervent faithfulness incomparable to all others, she discovered she could ask him to do anything and, miraculously, he would find a way to fulfill her wishes. So it was delicate Jane, so gentle and petite, who was in control of this mighty brute and his unlimited authority. But she respected his omnipotence through truthfulness and by listening to him with reverence for she knew mighty Jack, more than anything, desired honesty and wished to be understood.

If Jack and Jane had not chosen to work together, the widget shop would have failed. Or, should they have chosen to cooperate only partially, rather than completely, the widget shop would have struggled along in mediocrity. Because of the full marriage of their abilities, however, the widget shop, in spite of Earthly difficulties, became wonderfully successful.

Likewise, if our consciousness and subconsciousness are unbalanced, we will become a social nonentity. Or, if these coworkers of the mind are only partially balanced, we may, at times, be socially and intermittently bewildered. Yet, when we, from time to time, balance these two polar twins of the mind, we achieve an imperfect yet fairly consistent sense of well being. But it is important to note that these two parts of the mind are opposites. Their relationship is strikingly comparable to what is called *symbiosis* in which dissimilar organisms cooperate with some intimacy for mutual benefit. What is more, the marriage between the conscious and subconscious mind is not static but a rarified and fleeting series of consummations. Yet, the preeminence of these electrifying moments of intimacy allows deep penetration within the psyche apparatus having the potential to create change and newness.

This conflict of balance which impedes the distinction of our truest self is not easily resolved for it is fought by the most powerful forces on Earth—the conscious and subconscious mind. We have already visited some of their characteristics in our story about Jack and Jane, yet it may be helpful to consider them more closely.

The subconscious contains memories and repressed desires which are not subject to conscious perception but that often affect conscious thoughts and behavior.

It is the residence of childlike impulses we tend to turn our backs on as adults, the creator of our dreams at night, the child of wonder, the playful fascination of sex, the exuberance of delight. It is kaleidoscopic and thoroughly uninhibited. I suppose the subconscious is thought of as the mind of a newborn baby. It is primitive in this sense, wild. It possesses a singularity of logic which is unbiased and uncharacteristic of an adult and, perhaps most important to those who wish to achieve greatness, *no concept of impossibility.*

Inversely, the conscious mind is filled with ideas of what can and cannot be done. It is highly biased and maintains an array of taboos and inhibitions. It operates within the laws of the physical world and is keenly aware of and interested in reason, order, control and planning.

We must understand that creativity is the complimentary interplay of these two forces. Norman Podhertz said, "Creativity represents a miraculous coming together of the uninhibited energy of the child with its apparent opposite and enemy, the sense of order imposed by the disciplined adult intelligence."

So, their acrimonious nature must be appeased in some way; these two parts of the mind must be balanced and work together. To be powerful, in a beneficial manner, we must be attuned to them both. If we wall off the subconscious, we will not be able to enjoy anything. Turning off the subconscious is the cause of one being a wallflower at a dance, the boring, silent, non-contributor. The greater the polarization from subconsciousness, the greater is the self-alienation with antisocial and desensitizing results, albeit ever so mild or monstrous.

I believe the foremost symptom of this self-alienation of the subconscious is choosing the disliked while ignoring the liked. This encompasses an enormous sector of the world's population and in most cases, the justification for this behavior is so very logical and apparently well grounded it would prevail in a court of law. Those who would argue such a case are often extremely intelligent and possess an attractive personality yet have seldom or never experienced the mental balance we are discussing. It seems they have created a pseudo personality: one that they pretend to be so they will not be forced to see their real deficiencies—or more precisely, their real proficiencies; for it is their proficiencies, not their deficiencies, that truly frighten them. Consequently, they never take the risk of extending themselves to achieve anything or to experience the pain such a venture would entail. They live a safe, prosaic similitude of life yet their subconscious mind knows the truth: they possess greater abilities and are, therefore, a living contradiction. Should you feel this describes your present life, you will benefit from reading the remainder of this book with special attentiveness.

The subconscious mind might also be described as a powerful robot which submits to every beck and call of the conscious mind. It must follow the commands of our subconscious and in this way galvanizes our individual will. What is more, this mighty servant never, never forgets its commands—even the commands of a frightened child.

All of us experienced fright during the first crucial and formative six years of our childhood. Acclimating to a new world and a new body, neither of which we chose to live in, was traumatic; this new peculiar world of strange people and objects of colossal size was, at times, overwhelmingly frightful. Fragments of frightened childhood episodes may continue to live in a galvanized state within our subconscious; these cryptic fragments of our personality are surrounded by the walls we have cleverly constructed for we think these walls protect us from another episode of trauma.

In many cases this is true. But they can also be
blockades that prevent us from excellence in many
areas of our life and especially our work. A hallmark
of the well-adjusted adult is knowing when to retain
them for healthy boundaries and when to release them.
Of course, those adults who are maladjusted behave
more erratically: sometimes their boundaries are
guarded with puritanical virtue and at other times flung
away with ribald lust. So, these frightful childhood
experiences can be preserved for our safety but are just
as often used pretentiously. As time moves forward
and our bodies mature, we must regress further and
further backward into our childhood to re-experience
them as a womb called regression. Sadly, it is
impossible to grow spiritually, emotionally and fully
mature until these secret and protected holdings are
relinquished under the appropriate conditions; so,
unless dealt with properly, these hidden childhood
fears retard all growth. But how do we deal with them
properly?

When afraid as children, we may have given the
command of fearfulness to our subconscious minds
which, as you remember, never forgets a command.
There were probably justifiable reasons for this fear.
Maybe through the absence of love, validation and
respect for our lives we became terribly afraid of our

emotions. Later as adults, rather than choosing to deal with our fear, we found it easier to repress it thereby disallowing that segment of our childhood to mature. This is completely understandable since these very emotions may have been extremely enigmatic, even oblivious to us. But this allows the conscious and subconscious to become further and further apart. How can we deal with such emotions which are mysterious or of which we are unaware?

Inexorably our subconscious continues to obey its commands. Because the subconscious is omnipotent within the realm of our minds, our conscious mind materializes these commands even if it means contorting— yes, even perverting reality. Reality must be repressed in this way for the pain of these deepest emotions have become protected by plasticine instincts which are obeyed with unique primitiveness. Should we become aware of these childhood episodes, we cannot deal with them for they are too painful. It is debilitating. Thus, our awareness and "subawareness" become more alienated. This may be the root cause of neurosis.

In addition to perennial regression to our childhood that results in perennial infantilisms and adolescence, there are other ways to avoid our past. One of those ways is projection. Unwilling to identify childhood pain and fear as coming from within ourselves, we may sometimes project the pain and fear as coming from without. This is precisely what occurred throughout history, and what occurs today in some societies, during public executions. Often a former member of society was not only executed but scorned and ridicule was heaped upon him as the merciless crowd of onlookers projected *their own* wrongdoings upon the one convicted. Those sentenced to die became the scapegoat, the sacrificial lamb, as it were, in place of the wrongs that the crowd themselves may have committed. The members of the crowd, atop the pinnacle of hypocrisy, were unwilling to truthfully examine their own shortcomings but were perfectly willing to allow a subconscious outpouring of wrath upon someone else. So these compulsive-obsessive conditions are termed as *sharply split*—sharply split between what they subconsciously know about themselves and what is consciously concealed from themselves. Contrarians of their own wishes and diametrically opposed to their dreams of a better life, should they have any, they become fixated by repetitive thoughts which are often quite subtle and beguiling—a condition which virtually shuts down all creativity. Rather than confront the weaknesses within themselves, they hide from this inner truth which, therefore, must express itself as an aversion to others. But this self-alienation of those who are sharply split can also be expressed as intense desire in a projection of all that we perceive as being good, even saintly about ourselves. It is especially deep-felt when accompanied by sexual chemistry and *cathexis*, a bonding attachment of emotional longing. This is the reason so many people "fall in love" only to realize that, a few months later, the person with whom they've been smitten is far different from the idea they had projected into him or her. Their fickle desire then often becomes hate as they, once again, project their own self-hate into their former paramour. Within the mind of the sharply split, consequently, the entire Universe comprises only two shades: black and white, with little variation thereof.

Incidentally, the sharply split projection of love and hate creates another delusion: that love and hate are somehow intertwined so that love can quickly become hate. None of this is true. Love is the recognition of value. This does not suddenly change. So, it is far better to marry someone we deeply admire and in whom we needn't project fantasies. This is the way we ourselves wish to be loved, not with fickle, fanciful projections, which may just as easily become hate, but with genuine admiration and friendship.

We have been exploring the effects of ignoring some subconscious messages. But suppose one is attuned to the subconscious alone. What would then occur in the psyche? Such a person becomes schizophrenic losing all control, order and contact with reality. This condition is often characterized by seeing visions and hearing voices. Schizophrenia is beyond the scope of this book. Anyone with such symptoms must immediately seek the aid of a psychiatrist.

So these two parts of the mind, the civilized and primordial, are, *ideally*, designed to function together. Yet, they are simultaneously like two magnets with opposing fields of energy. They repel. This natural repelling with only transitory alliances is why the story of Jack and Jane began with the words, *"Once upon a fleeting moment—yes, all in a fleeting moment sparkling so brightly . . ."* Their synchronicity is fleeting and limited to varying degrees.

But, their occasional interconnectedness is the affirmation of a primarily healthy personality; and, as we have seen, this complimentary alliance of the child and the adult is the basis of the creator, the individual who is unafraid to try something eccentric yet, because of uninhibited creativity, will also find a method of implementation. As a harmony of these two conscious modules occur, they each function differently, compensating for their mutual deficiencies and filling the other's void, very similar to symbiosis. The liveliness of a child with the maturity of an adult evolves so that this optimal creativity is simultaneously flowing yet methodical; the personality becomes, at once, mature yet youthful, orderly yet imaginative and the result is equanimity. This is the adult appropriately *at play*; and, this is psychosynthesis: the equilibrium of the conscious and the subconscious mind.

This intersection is the province of genius. British intellectual Bernard Berenson seemed to understand this, as well. He said, "We define genius as the capacity for productive reaction against one's training." In other words, we maintain a childlike "experimentality" while respecting realism yet being unencumbered by it. We then begin to see that limitations are often artificial while accepting the facts that the conscious presents to us; we embrace the limitless possibilities of the subconscious and, contemporaneously, the limited possibilities of the conscious. The result is a very, very positive person living in reality. This mutual allegiance is the only way we express our genius. It is then that we transcend the contradiction of our personhood. Then we are fully alive, using all our gifts, all our faculties in a fluorescence of life. This is why Italian novelist Ceasre Pavese said, "To be a genius is to achieve complete possession of one's own experience, body, rhythm and memories." This is a beautiful description of the mind at balance.

We may further describe this childlike yet adult state—this methodical yet flowing state—by considering Picasso's idea of Cubism. In Cubism we have what I call *form without conformity*; in other words, Cubism is a clearly defined art *form,* yet its creation was not an act of *conformity* but one of unique invention. But many people have been miss-inspired by Cubism to create a pseudo-modernity by doing the very opposite of Picasso. They present *no* form *with* conformity. They assumed anything is art and therefore conform to the *status quo* with the pretension of being *avant garde.* Thus we have *l' enfant terrible* which is a term referring to art created by the infantile subconscious minus conscious adulthood. The result is art that could have been created by an infant in his "terrible twos."

Art, on the other hand, is a unique combining and balancing of the inhibited and uninhibited mind. We wish to bring the adult and the child together in harmony. This, however, is a rarity. A battle exists between them.

Yet, suppose this *gigantomachy*—this battle of the civilized and uncivilized giants, the inhibited and uninhibited giants—could be replaced with episodes of harmony.

Mastery of the Unfulfilled Wish

Now that we have a rudimentary understanding of the roles played by the surface and submerged mind, we will progress from that simple concept to those more complex.

Our deepest wish—the unfulfilled wish resides in each of us and, far beyond all other human assets, is our greatest power. Yet, within the masses, these life-struggles manifest a cry of muddled imbroglio without echo or response across a silent, starlit desert. Should we but attune ourselves to their subtleties, we distinguish one urgent, sub vocal message. We hear it within the newborn's awakening gasp of air, man's inexorable primal roar and the faint whisper of the dying self, *"Injustice! I am here . . . I posses value!"*

Mastery of this wish is, indeed, the jeweled key to the ever moving life-stream wherein which these pell mell yearnings symphonize to become art.

But how could we possibly master such a thing as an unfulfilled wish?

The subliminal matrix that all of us acquired during

infancy, manifesting throughout the length and the breadth of our lives, sometimes positively, sometimes negatively, is commonly accepted as an unfulfilled wish. Because this wish resides within the subconscious, we know it has at its disposal unlimited authority and consistently imposes its sovereignty upon the conscious. Of course, this why we sometimes wonder at our behavior as though it were foreign; the unfulfilled wish, or at least its facsimile, always manifest itself in the material world.

Now, suppose that, although it may predominate portions of our life, the wish to control others was not the preeminent wish within our subconscious? Imagine, if you will, that there was another wish inherently powered by a magnificent, inexhaustible desire, the satisfying of which produced unparalleled gratification? Suppose this wish fulfillment was holistically dynamic, subordinating all other wishes within the subconscious, providing the background for personality reordering and, therefore, psychogenic awakening—the experiential realization of self-value?

What if this specific life-wish or *vita-wish*, as I call it, was by nature all consuming, complimented with the ability to affect some neurotic behavior *without conscious deliberation?*

To be sure, there *is* a desire which is largely untapped within our subconscious; while it is not by any means a panacea, the vita-wish can create enormous good among us as we individually seek its fulfillment; for the profundity of its influence upon the lessor wishes, surfacing as neurotic behavior, has a governing effect upon them. These lessor wishes are utterly opposed to the vita-wish, continually, simultaneously creating multiple distractions. That is why I refer to them as a death-wish or *necro-wish*. Necros are functional inhibitors; that is, they produce dysfunction, reproducing inhibitory details within our minds, preventing us from moving toward completion or the condition of being fully alive. This is the rudimentary cause of procrastination, and, *procrastination is rehearsal for death.*

It is important to note, by the way, that the author attributes human qualities in anthropomorphic terms to describe the vita-wish and necro-wish. This projection of human characteristics, it is hoped, will make it easier to understand their nature. But they are not little people; nor are they living things or organisms. Vita and necro are merely labels I have given to positive and negative memories and thinking. They can, however, seem to take on a life of their own when not given the proper tasks. Now, wouldn't it be wonderful if we beheld that golden task right before us?

The vita-necro inter-dynamics remarkably parallel events which are said to have happened in Twelfth Century Switzerland. The Swiss people were fighting for their freedom against the oppressive rule of the Austrians; and the Swiss Guard, a faithful breed of men whose nobility formed a defiance seemingly unmatched by the well-trained Austrian military, were so resolutely united that Austria feared it would be impossible to rule them much longer.

Then the Austrians conceived a plan. Since the Swiss were so formidable a foe to oppose from without, why not oppose them from within? While devising this plan, their reconnaissance spies made a remarkable discovery: an entire company of Swiss Guards had been killed in combat, yet their fatalities were, as of then, unreported. If a few members of this lost company could be impersonated, the Swiss Guard could be successfully infiltrated with Austrian troops.

The plan was instigated flawlessly.

Austrian troops in tattered uniforms of the Swiss Guard and feigning battle weariness as though they were returning from the front lines, had the intent of dispersing into several different companies. But on the second day of their secret occupation, they were mustered in formation to receive thanks for their valiant service from Arnold von Lucerene, a knight of the Unterwalden and Swiss Guard Commandant. His irresistible, charismatic powers mixed with humility and kindness, considerations to which they were unaccustomed, magnetized the men and within a few days they were persuaded to Swiss allegiance. The Austrian officer in charge of the mole operation confessed their plot of espionage and, along with his men, offered to fight to their last drop of blood for the Swiss Guard.

Likewise, the average person's subconscious has been infiltrated by unfriendly forces which must be won over by an empowered vita, just as Arnold von Lucerene won over the Austrian infiltrators.

Incidentally, I only use this story illustratively. The Austrian people were warm and hospitable to me on my visits there and I hope to return soon. I love stunningly beautiful Austria and her equally beautiful people.

While the story of Arnold von Lucern is helpful in understanding the vita-necro conflict, the drama of our lives takes place before the backdrop of the vexing human condition where the complexities of our struggle are much more intense for we progressively struggle from the point at which the vita is altogether primitive. Indeed, we needn't teach our children to lie. They expertly make this discovery upon their own. We do, by contrast, need to teach them to tell the truth. Furthermore, though we plant grass, shrubs, flowers and cultivate their growth, we never plant weeds or fertilize them should they appear; they simply appear in our garden, like the Austrian infiltrators, and we try to control them. Similarly, the vita-wish must be discovered, nurtured and developed; whereas, the necro-wishes, and sometimes there are many of them, infiltrate and exist within most of us in varying degrees but thrive unopposed like weeds in the mentally ill.

Indeed, the necros retard growth within the host mind and, without conscious knowledge of the host, implant the same retarding mechanisms within the mind of those who come in contact with them. They lose contagiousness in most day-to-day encounters, reduced to mostly annoying others. Yet, they can spawn a subliminal matrix with equal potency in those who have not been inoculated with a strong vita, a role exquisitely played by Commandant Arnold von Lucerene; and, of course, fertility for the necro matrix is found within the infantile mind of any age but particularly minors and the mentally disturbed. Thus, with a very similar counterespionage as the Austrians attempted, the necro is an infectious psyche disease which, when not under the auspices of the vita, may ravage through relationships and organizations with breathtaking speed and, before the naked conscious mind, is an unstoppable juggernaut of savage devastation.

Again, the necro-wishes are secretive in nature, usually unknown to our conscious, absorbing energy, as all secrets do, in an attempt to influence the conscious without its detection. Upon their rarefied discovery, these trespassers occasionally appear to have been overcome by the hosts painstaking efforts until the exasperating discovery is made that they have merely retreated into a regressive state; and although they may be discovered in glimpses, they remain enigmatic, elusive, as if they had a life of their own, momentarily staring out at us, figuratively speaking, from within the oblique nature of the subconscious in an unrepentant gloating, assured of their impenetrable position within the most powerful force in the mental universe. These are merely suppressed memories, feelings and experiences. Nonetheless, the necro-matrix—so stealthy an intertwining—can net our subconscious, tightly enmeshing our struggle for mobility from infancy into adolescence and toward adulthood; and, necros residing in others with poor mental hygiene will, unquestionably, discourage us from escaping the necro dictatorship, enabling, encouraging, insisting that we remain under their tyranny, but only with our varnished conscious. To be sure, they are impervious to our conscious attempts of rehabilitation for no conscious weapon formed will prosper against the forces of the subconscious. The subconscious always has its way.

So, this civil war of the vita and necros within the subconscious wages on and on, largely unbeknownst or, should it be discovered, misunderstood by the host; it is only known that something is wrong; and, so the mysteries of man's behavior swirl within this secret storm eviscerating the life from within our breasts wherein which we so often feel a void. Some of us plod in a directionless groping, pursuing an almost inexplicable association of thoughts until the discovery of the life-wish.

Then bolted double locks are burst asunder and doors flung wide, opening us to that most intrepid life force—true love. And how is this to be done? Must we find someone with whom to fall in love? Precisely. We must find someone. When we do, we shall fall in love. This crypticness is intended to inspire thought and will be plainly decoded later.

Fortunately, within each of us is this *ultimus optatum* or ultimate wish. This supreme wish, the vita, possesses no concept of impossibility. It disregards the impossible since it dwells and operates within the realm of the subconscious—the sequential, perennial caretaker, age upon age, of original thought.

The vita is, therefore, incessantly prolific without limitation; for consciousness is merely a deterring anomaly and at other times an appropriate filter to this vast, super engine.

To fathom the magnetic grandeur of the vita and its irresistible effect upon the necros, consider the Maslowian Needs. From the lowest to the highest they are:

>safety
>nourishment
>sex
>sociability
>self-actualization

We are powerfully driven to satisfy these needs and very few things will or can stand in the way of someone who seeks their satisfaction. Now consider this: all these needs are driven by the vita. Yes, the vita is, unquestionably, life's dynamo.

Upon the satisfaction of each of the Maslowian Needs, the next need becomes dominant; the vita is then ready for its next assignment within the hierarchy of needs. Notwithstanding, the last stage of self-actualization is met with some trepidation for its attainment is, of course, more complex than the attainment of safety and food; and, the threshold of self-actualization, thought to be the satisfaction of the human predicament, is where most of us stop or experience impeding frustration. The vita has done its job. Once again it has led us to survival and, if it is not given further specific, co-direction from the conscious and subconscious, our lives will be partially, rather than fully, experienced. The ulterior motives within the subconscious, specifically, the necro-wishes, instigate a disruptive distraction from our life-wish, commandeering the subconscious and the vita itself. Moreover, if the vita is fraught with "directionlessness" and, consequently, without the ability to govern its domain with autocracy, the ever present necros are free to cause confusion within the subconscious, at times surfacing as neurosis.

So, the host mind, inhabited by the ungoverned necros, is in a continuous state of insurrection, unable to experience balance and, therefore, direction; what is more, should the host know only of this unsettled state, especially if it feels normal to the host, it persists as normalcy unaware of something better—the elixir of life—the full presence of the vita. From this place of unrest, the host inevitably seeks animation from others rather than discovering, nurturing and developing liveliness within itself. This pecking order, so to speak, materializes in the world around us and is nothing more than social dynamics and, if it is benevolently implemented, is the quintessence of leadership. We all look to the one with the most power to lead us.

Albeit, should the vita be underdeveloped or worse, unrecognized, within the host, its vulnerable yet magnetic-energy will be an irresistible source of life for the psyche parasites; very similar to a carnivorous animal which carefully selects and stalks its prey that is weak enough to be overpowered yet strong enough to give it life, the co-dependent subconscious, dominated by necros, will neurotically seek a vessel for psyche inhabitation. Through congenital or organic imbalances sometime this wish for vicarious fulfillment is compelling enough to become quite deliberate with subversive, malicious expectation —psychosis—a malady far beyond the scope of our inquiry. Psychiatric help must be sought immediately for such matters.

Unlike psychosis, conscious deliberation to adjust neurotic maladies is good, to be sure. Yet, it is often a suppressive endeavor, the focus of which, and therefore the energy of which, is given to the necros. Therapists typically focus upon the problem rather than the solution. And, in this process, should the necros be temporarily overcome, an appropriate, stronger substitute is commonly not introduced by the traditionalist counselor.

To clearly understand this grand mistake, imagine, if you will, the incandescent countenance of adoration emanating toward you from the face of someone you love with equal glowing desire. Blending effortlessly, the variegated embroideries of your two individuated personalities become one.

Now, suppose that an invisible force compelled you to see someone else whose presence instantly filled you with boredom. Begrudgingly, again and again you acquiesce to this superior force, forsaking your true love, enduring the absence of electrochemistry which only first love stimulates.

What would become of your disposition? Most people would be depressed, apathetic, despondent. Lost love becomes lost hope. Many times it crushes animation to death. Notwithstanding all the psychoneurological considerations, this little story of fulfilled and unfulfilled love is fairly representational of all depression, apathy and despondency.

The grand mistake is the psyche embrace of the unlovely rather than the lovely. And, the grand question which we shall answer is: *What is the first love that we should psychologically embrace?*

Many necros may coexist with the vita, although their coexistence is organized by the dominant or subservient position of the vita; the vita's numerous roles may vary and its position, whether king, lord, republican or slave, to the necros is evident in our mental equilibrium. The experience of being fully alive, fully human is enjoyed by those whose vita is supreme master of the subconscious and in which the necros are obedient subjects serving or remaining somewhat dormant with the precincts of the vita's realm.

To further illustrate the authoritativeness of the vita upon necros, it is helpful to think of the human condition when the lower Maslowian Needs are dominant: during this time, the necros are usually well behaved; they step aside, so to speak, for the intensely motivated vita to acquire safety and food. Not only does this example of the necro's obedience tell us that they are *weak* before the vita, it is also a telling example of the necro's *obsequious nature* before the undivided motivation of the vita. The necros let the vita have its uncontested prerogative "to let the spiritual, unbidden and unconscious, grow up through the common," as William Ellery Channing wrote in, *My Symphony*.

This occurs super-consciously, super-therapeutically. It is liberating to know the truth: the necros can be dominated *without conscious deliberation*. Yes, if the necros acquiesce before the vita as it presents the need for safety and food, it will continue its obedience as the vita presents another compelling reason for the necro's subjugation—a phenomenon which we will clearly describe in the following pages.

So, after the basic survival needs have been met, the vita, if used correctly or, more precisely, allowed to flourish, will reorder the psyche by drawing power unto itself.

I remember when, during recess at grade school, a dozen boys and I would play king-of-the-mountain. But to make our game truly exciting, we would play it on the merry-go-round. We would begin by running along its sides, speeding its rotation so fast that we could barely jump on. Then, with a profusion of laughter, our spiraling, dizzying king-of-the-mountain began. Centrifugal force pushed the weaker of us away from the center and the stronger of us took even more strength from the others as we pushed them backwards. Whoever could remain in the center was king. Likewise, and figuratively speaking, the vita centrifugally repels the necros while centripetally repossessing energy from them, the vita hierarchy once again being prioritized by a definite and strong vita. This is the normal, although not average, function of the mind.

Of course, there are cases, such as severe retardation, schizophrenia and organic psychosis, where the unbridled subconscious is partly oblivious even to the need of safety and food and, consequently, oblivious to the vita. Yet, while these people are beyond the sphere of psychosynthesis' therapeutic influence, others dealing with neurosis may find that, while it alone will not conquer emotional or mental problems, it, nevertheless, may be helpful.

Even slight helpfulness, however, is important because we know so little about dealing with the subconscious. For conscious adjustments to the subconscious are habitually acts of mild to severe ignorance, cruelty or both as we neurotically command ourselves to contradict our subliminal natures. In fact, one of the most popular, contemporary psychologists grabs patients by the shoulders, shakes them violently and screams in their face before a large audience. I wonder if conscious equilibrium is achieved by this method?

Obviously, a finer method must be found to resolve the conflict between the conscious and subconscious. The irrationality of these polar twins is like two lovers reluctant to give themselves completely to the other. Should they resolve the conflict, a fabulous climax followed by blissful harmony would ensue. They know they have a conflict. They also know that should they discover an antidote, their problems will not disappear but may be controlled. So it is with our minds: it is not so much the presence of the necros as it is the absence of a solution—*a motive for the vita*. When the correct motive is presented to the vita, protocol is created between the two conscious'. Rather than with ignorance and cruelty, the vita presides with intelligence and magnanimity over the conscious and subconscious. A balanced sense of well being is enjoyed, namely, *homeostasis*. It is comfortable, benevolent, dignified.

Once again, it is critical to achieve the appropriate hierarchy of the vita—its dominance—in contrast to the end result of some psychologic solutions. Traditionally speaking, these solutions inadvertently give energy to the necros by singularly focusing upon them and creating a teleological effect within the patient's mind drawing them toward the problem rather than its solution; in this manner, the hierarchy is inverted and, often the precise miscarriage of mental health is accomplished.

Each of us who drives a car has undoubtedly experienced a similar phenomenon. While driving along a narrow two-lane street, if we look at the car next to us we will unwittingly steer in that direction. For this reason, driving schools instruct their students to focus on the road before them rather than the objects, like a tree, they wish to avoid. It is a simple yet essential lesson, although opaque to a small group in the field of counseling. Indeed, there is value in knowing that the necros are there and, perhaps, what caused them and their effect upon us; yet, it is equally valuable to know that we are incapable of erasing them and, furthermore, that we are incapable of controlling them with our conscious mind by willfulness or by conscious deliberation; if we do not come to this life-altering conclusion, we will invariably and neurotically force ourselves to attempt the impossible—to change ourselves—leading to yet more neurosis.

Of course, we must understand our problems and that understanding requires some focus and some conscious deliberation. So, I am not suggesting that people stop trying. I am not suggesting, for instance, that people no longer attend Alcoholic Anonymous meetings. I am, however, suggesting that we are uniquely limited in affecting the subconscious. Jane Conscious was able to affect Jack Subconscious to a degree purely because she was using a method we have yet to discuss. Without that method, the subconscious is like another planet to us.

For instance, the Rolls Royce is possibly the finest production car in the world and fully appropriate to motor around metropolitan Earth; therefore, should we presume it might be appropriate to be launched in a space shuttle to the Moon and driven along the lunar surface? Conscious solutions are equally inappropriate for the subconscious mind. Thus, as we diligently work within the perimeters of the conscious world, our only place of conscious jurisdiction, the vita will automatically, expertly perform its work in a place

where we can never work effectively, no more than a
Rolls Royce is an effective extraterrestrial vehicle; for
in a labyrinthine environment which is foreign to us,
the climate of which is unpredictable, even hostile,
wherein the terrain is impossibly rugged and the
native's will nonnegotiable, the vita, nonetheless,
commands its dominion with unlimited authority. It
rules the subconscious.

Indeed, the inner world of our mind is the variegated,
fluid, ever-changing, infinite-sided mobile wherein
there is neither work nor monotony. This is a true yet
obviously incomplete description of the inner mind; it
will always elude complete description since
something describing itself is incapable of objectivity.
We may have quasi-verifications or a verisimilitude
but never, never anything approaching its complete
vision. In *Doors of Perception*, Aldous Huxley said,
"All that the conscious ego can do is to formulate
wishes, which it controls very little and understands
not at all. We visit it only in dreams and muslings, and
its strangeness is such that we never find the same
world on two occasions."

But what if we could formulate wishes that we, in turn,
expertly controlled and clearly understood? What

would be the implications if we could daily visit this inner world, not only in dreams and muslings, but in a way which harnessed and then mobilized those visceral wishes? Suppose this phenomenon could be formulaic? Suppose it could become the near-perfect gratification of our unfulfilled wish—the complete use of ourselves? What, then, would be possible for us to achieve?

These suppositions lead to something much more powerful than positive thinking. Of course, we can compensate by choosing a positive mentality but, nonetheless, project nonsuccess with chronic disappointment into our world because the necro-wishes, the death-wishes remain unrestrained anarchists. This illuminates the fallacy of most motivation which is composed of transitory excitation rather than a teleological motivation that always completes itself. Negligent sufferings, vain sufferings, caused by such misdirected hope breaks the hearts of multitudes simply because the necros mysteriously, secretly ravage the mind although positive thinking is heroically attempted.

Imagine if it were different. Imagine if all of life's memories, those which are conscious and subconscious, including the necros, could be marshaled to form a precision instrument fashioned from a psyche-energy, capable of channeling the undivided power of the vita.

The Struggle for Completion

Our completion will be a struggle for these reasons: the etherealness of the fulfilled wish remains with us, even exudes from us and rhythmically vaporizes like the morning mists. Should its experience be evergreen, its novel pleasure would not be comparably good for it would have no opposites and, therefore, nothingness, a purely hypothetical, impossible realm would exist or, non-exist. For to experience fulfillment we must constantly have, in seamless flow, comparisons, associations, benchmarks; without them fulfillment does not exist; and we can see, rather obviously then, that the word incomparable is an oxymoron. Should we experience life, rather than it absence, it is done with motion as we move toward completion while wittingly and unwittingly comparing that from which we have moved. Our work, then, is to make continuous, appropriate adjustments as we embrace and seek the elusive. Fulfillment is experienced within the context of nonfulfillment. But this pursuit is not drudgery. We are more than, as Dickens said, "fellow passengers to the grave." While fully appreciating Dickens' compassionate subtleties, we are not only born in a cavalcade of dullness but also vibrancy, fatigue but also energy, defeat but also victory, all of which are those hallmarks of being fully alive. Completion is the object. We must work and struggle to attain it. All of us, however, tend to pursue self-transcendence without completion since transcending our self is by far the easier of the two.

Throughout the *Odyssey*, Homer repeatedly referred to its protagonist as "longsuffering Odysseus." Suffer he did, seeking the completion of his twenty-year military expedition and wanderings, enduring manifold, hideous hardships, some by miscalculation others by the malevolent providence of Poseidon on his arduous return to Ithaca and Penelope. He did not try to transcend his pain-filled, yearning love for Ithaca and Penelope. He completed his love for them by progressive struggling. Homer's crystalline message: we too will endure much suffering in our quest for completion.

Like Odysseus, the competent are those who are willing to suffer but not, of course, for the sake of suffering itself. They, instead, suffer for the experience of non-contradiction, that rare condition, that solid state so often called integrity which is the ultimate alternative lifestyle; it is telling the truth to ourselves, especially in valuing our abilities, and telling the truth to others in practical, day-to-day circumstances. This longsuffering is more than our willingness to deal with facts. It is the act of agreeing with them. It is a longsuffering that agrees with the facts, not as we wish them to be, but as they exist in their ice cold condition. In this respect, non-contradiction is a synonym of competence.

We admire Odysseus for many reasons yet I feel this is the primary one: he suffered magnificently as we often suffer alone in silence and so he becomes special kin to us for he overcame his hideous trials through versatility and longsuffering in ways that succeeded. He could have remained with mesmerically beautiful Calypso in her garden island. He could have remained with equally beautiful Circe in idylls of splendor. Rather, he chose Ithaca and Penelope and we love him for this. Why? Should he have remained in either of these new lands with new wives, would we not love him still? No, we would not. If he did so, he would not have completed himself. Self completion, although it is painful, is singularly why Odysseus is the worthiest of heros.

He, who with clarity of conscious, needn't deflect his calm, beneficial gaze from human countenance, has neither turned away from manly suffering.

On the other hand, any act of laziness, which is the refusal to suffer appropriately, betrays the vita and, over time, sickens it and allows it to be swarmed by necros. Evilness is the condition of excessive laziness. There exists no other state which renders such nonfulfillment. Thus, for fulfillment, there is suffering. There is struggle for completion.

The genius is sometimes organically, sometimes socially predisposed to this struggle toward completion; for, the single act which evokes man's uttermost mystical energies, the spiritual salvation which transforms his torment into art and reintroduces mankind to the threshold of the Garden is to *think*. Moreover, exorbitant thinking—this most rare genre of thinking which enlarges the boundaries of the human realm—can be induced although it may not have been randomly inherited from the gene pool or incubated socially. For within the subconscious mind of the normal human being is the point of supreme human power, the vita-wish, within which are the elements of genius. Indeed, vita-powered-thinking is the province of genius.

Synopsis of the Unfulfilled Wish

At this point, it may be helpful to, very briefly, recapitulate what we have covered thus far:

The surfaced and submerged minds exist in simultaneous need and enmity of one another. It is analogous to a symbiotic relationship, but many times more complex, for in symbiosis two dissimilar organisms cooperate without enmity and in total receptivity. Yet, in the conundrum of the human mind, we must work midst an ongoing conflict with the hope of achieving only intermittent cooperation and sometimes only in fleeting moments. What is more, we possess limited understanding of the surfaced mind and even less of the submerged which, to further intensify the equation, is more powerful beyond measure than the surfaced. This conflict and complexity of the mind cannot be managed with conscious effort. It can only be managed by opening the subconscious to a dialog upon its own terms. This is achieved without conscious deliberation and by the supereminence of the vita.

Yet, to accurately portray the fulfillment of the unfulfilled wish, we must be completely honest. Although we may enjoy the imperialism of the vita, we will yet struggle for our completion.

The Fulfilled Wish

IMAGINE THAT A WELL-KNOWN philharmonic company is losing its balance. Within six months, two conductors resigned leaving a leadership void and the legacy of a highly politicized organization. Other than the desire to produce great music, even the musicians, it seems, have little in common but mutual animosity and intense frustration.

Amidst their fraternal chaos, they hear a tapping at the podium. Now unified by hushed, breathtaking astonishment they recognize a man with silver mane which seems to form an aura of energy crowning his ruddy complexion further accented by a black turtle-neck sweater. His slender, athletic physic and commanding movements exude self assuredness filling the space he occupies and the entire concert hall with the wealth of his incontestable virtuosity.

"Good morning," he says cheerily. "The director was to be here today to introduce us but was taken ill. So, if I may. I'll introduce myself and then I want to met each of you. My name is Leonard Bernstein."

Forgetting their "triflings" that morning, they performed Rachmaninoff's *Rhapsody on a Theme of Paganini* with unprecedented, sublime elegance.

It is similar that the vita orchestrates the tone and rhythm of our life-events as a maestro conductor so that none of our life experiences are in vain; all are fuels for the vita super-engine. We begin to hear and then listen to the vita as it psychically resonates a story of peculiar familiarity yet one to which we were previously deaf—our autobiography. We then begin to believe what was true all along about ourselves but which was too frightfully good to accept.

Without conscious deliberation the irreducible objectives of psychoanalysis and psychotherapy subtlety begins—the balance of the conscious and subconscious mind: the performance of our undivided self, the fluorescence of life, the discovery of the quintessential expression of our original self, at once, vessel and vehicle of the vita.

The most intelligent use of ourselves is discovered— the full use of our talent—for our talent is the precise fulfillment of the unfulfilled wish.

Subconsciously formulated as talent the superordin-ate vita-wish unleashes the dual forces of suppressed wishes—necros—and the wish for unbridled life— the primal vita-wish. The suppressed secrets of the subconscious, little by little, yet sometimes in the twinkling of an eye, can now, perhaps for the first time, be countenanced because each event, even the darkest, has become an instrument of our life-force. Now, as a by-product of the unfettered use of our talent, we are correspondingly willing to, little by little, plumb our own depths, to dig into the innermost recesses of our personality with equal energy to which we pursue our talent. The necros begin to cease their political, fraternal strife as the centrifugal force of the vita slowly creates a prioritized orbit of every past event, whether good or bad, revolving in a circle of planetary balance. The coalescence of each life-event marshaled under the generalship of the vita, formulated as our talent, formulated as our true self, inexorably moves toward life.

To be sure, talent is the superconductor of the vita. It is the centerpiece of psychosynthesis and the psychological elegance of talent along with its foundation, the integration of truthfulness, perhaps more accurately described as non-contradiction, throughout our personal and professional lives; for talent in motion is quintessential non-contradiction.

Yet, life remains a challenge. Ascendancy of the common man is fraught with many struggles. The grandeur of a cathedral protected by precipitous precinct walls wherein which the highest honor is bestowed upon men blatantly contrasts his all but anonymous life often endured in poverty. And, within the minds of his peasant contemporaries, as much as they want their daily bread, they want their mediocrity and cherish every attempt to vicariously impose it upon him. So, although he is uniquely gifted, merely finding his lot in life can batter him to his knees. But, if he is wise, in the midst of his life-struggles he knows this: his coronation, jubilated within a realm without subjects or the visible majesty of a monarch, nevertheless, is completed with a crown. For there is a path to these heights, an arduous but true path and one to which we are welcomed.

We will visit this very path in the following pages as we consider what might be some, but surely not all, of the experiential hallmarks of talent to which Everyman is welcomed.

Quietness followed by motion:

As Thomas Gray wrote in *Elegy Written in a Country Churchyard,* there is a quietness we should seek, "far from the madding crowd's ignoble strife." Many of the answers we seek are to be found there. Our subconscious is always seeking the opportunity to express itself should we only be willing to listen to its important messages. It is often in stillness that we discover the talent that best orchestrates our comprehensive life events. Quietness accentuates creativity. It calms the contradictious issues that seem to impose upon our essential thoughts. Tranquility genders tranquility. It purifies. It renews. In a reunion of what has been dissipated by the banter of the day, quietness reorders the multiple combinations of eight billion bits of data within our cerebral biocomputer. Yet, on how many occasions have we, in relaxation, experienced the absence of sound? Some are afraid of the settling therapy for which our mind most yearns. Silence may be the beginning for those who wish to discover their talent. "In quietness and confidence shall be thy strength." Quietness is often a prime tool of the creative mind. Quiet is a mirror of the mind, a moment of truth revealing our self-comfort or discomfort and, if we have them, possibly our neuroses. And what could be more neurotic than to distance ourselves from our own thoughts by electronic sights and sounds?

Ascendancy of the vita begins, it seems, in quiet. Yet, sometimes quietness can, in fact be accompanied by sound; many people feel that listening to great music such as the melodic works of Mozart can lift creativity. At other times, the profundity of inner quiet is accentuated in the midst of both vigorous noise and motion: after interminably long hours of research conducted in an utterly silent, pristine laboratory, physicist Leo Szilard had not discovered the mysteries for which he sought; mysteries that would change the world. Not until he was caught in a cacophony of traffic blare midst a swirl of human hustle crossing Southhampton Row in London did the concept of nuclear chain reaction brilliantly arise within his conscious. Amongst that higglely-pigglely clatter and commotion, the answer was stunningly obvious. So, although it may be surrounded by a discombobulated environment, inner quiet is the habitat of creation. Nevertheless, it seems genuine silence and stillness is an indispensable tool of creativity.

Those who have made the profound discovery of talent in quietness know that quietness is followed in tandem by motion. Talent inspires movement of the highest animation, our true choreography of life.

One evening I had dinner with a ballerina and afterwards attended a ballet where I was introduced to the genius of Twyla Thorpe. My date's enthusiasm for Twyla, whom she extolled as "the finest dance choreographer in the world," was later shared as we witnessed abundant life in the form of a ballet titled, *In the Upper Room.* Five thousand people were in attendance that night and at the end of Ms. Thorpe's triumph, I jumped to my feet, thrust my fist in the air and shouted, *"Yeah!"* It was simply too good for a trifling *Bravo!* Fortunately, I was not alone. For almost fifteen minutes the entire house lauded a standing ovation of cheers, whistling and thunderous applause upon the performers. I believe the rich, lyrical fluidity and explosive volcanic power of Ms. Thorpe's masterpiece was born while listening to her still, small inner voice singularly heard within the sanctuary of quietness. Indeed, vigorous motion is typically followed by this non-contradictious and quiet contemplation of our talent.

Industriousness

When celebrating the triumph of reconciling the dichotomy of the need to labor and our original self, a reconciliation we call talent, we are unlikely to wish the party to end.

Most of us have been at a party or get-together of sorts that was so refreshing and free that we didn't want to leave. In some cases, such a party may go on for many hours beyond expectation and into the morning. For this same reason, those who have discovered their talent are vigorously industrious. They have discovered their game. They have discovered their correct way of playing. The work of our talent is, thus, joyful.

This does not imply that we should be giggling all the time. There will be many times when working at our talent will be plain hard work which is tedious and frustrating and disappointed by delays. We may finally feel like giving up. We may have tried for so long without success that we break down in sobbing tears. A time of recreation for a half day, two days or week or more may be needed. Yet, there will be an underlying joy attached to our talent for we have the prospect of possessing our sweetest desire.

What I call *self-cathexis*, or the investment of mental and emotional energy into our near and distant past, is a unique attachment to our original self. It is, without conscious deliberation, dealing with, reconciling and holding all that we have been. This is why others may be amazed that one who works at his talent can appear to be almost punishing himself by working long, long hours in uninterrupted concentration. Sometimes they see the hard labor but not the wanderlust that beckons.

Auto-Therapy

In this section, we will not discuss how auto-therapy works for that has been discussed throughly in our discourse about vita-necro dynamics. There are, however, a few points here about auto-therapy which the reader may value.

Some may legitimately question the profundity of talent's effect upon the mind, particularly assuming that many people use their talent yet are subsequently unhappy. A quasi-laboratory of such an inquiry could be the cinematography industry where a psychological compliment to talent is, in many cases, one of personal unhappiness—a clear indication of an unfulfilled wish. But merely because actors and actresses are in a film does not imply they have used, or ever will use, their talent to the uttermost. Nor does it mean they are living truthfully toward themselves or others.

Now, with the caveat that we will struggle at times, think of the ability to, indirectly yet appropriately, deal with all our past emotional problems.

Think of the ability to do this effortlessly.

What would that feel like?

Recall the story you read in the introduction of this book. As you remember, you were asked to reminisce about your experience in the first grade. You were asked to imagine being kept indoors the entire school year when the other children were allowed to play at recess. This was a tragically sad story.

Now imagine, after having been kept indoors the entire school year, being released to run out onto the playground on a bright Spring day where all your friends excitedly cheered and ran to welcome you.

Everyone ran across the playground together and you were the fastest. You slid into home plate and the dirt flew in the air. You climbed the Jungle Gym faster and higher than anyone. You laughed until your stomach ached. All your friends followed you when you led to the charge into battle.

Imagine having this experience over and over again simply by using your talent.

That is how auto-therapy feels.

Humility

One of the best-known athletes in the world is an almost miraculously talented tennis player. He is young, handsome, cultured and wealthy. Yet, the attribute that magnetizes the masses unto him is his humility. He drives an inexpensive car, dresses conservatively and does not flaunt his fame and fortune. His self-statement is compartmentalized in his astonishing tennis playing wherein he presents his true self. He has no need to be arrogant. After all, arrogance is always and only a pretense, a facade intended to hide inadequacies. What is more, his humility provides a benefit beyond his magnetism. His humility compartmentalizes all his energies into playing tennis. If he were arrogant, he would inadvertently subtract energy from his performance.

Contrariwise is the attitude of a friend of mine who was also young and handsome. He drove an expensive roadster, lived in a beautiful home, wore beautiful clothes and dated beautiful women. He was sincere but he was fearfully lost without knowing his talent. This caused his insecurities and corresponding pretense of confidence that others knew as arrogance. He was without direction and eventually, as a consequence, without energy.

So we come to a critical truism of our subject: *humility energizes the performance of our talent.*

Yes, should we use our talent to bring attention to ourselves, its therapeutic value is all but lost and the ascendancy to our talent's pinnacle, it seems, would be improbable. Ego aggrandizement limits the full expression of our talent; for should our talent be truly sublime, it cannot be performed purely for *us* since we are simply not big enough for the product of the super-engine that is our own talent. Neither can we fully release our talent if we are its principal beneficiary for we cannot possibly contain its completeness. Indeed, the essence of self-perfidy is denying the release and full expression of our wishes, past and present which is small thinking at best, and at worst, a sort of subliminal masochism.

We have many reasons to be humble. Regardless of any greatness that may be attained, we are only "sunlight fading in the grass." We are beneficiaries of immensely talented people who have gone before us bequeathing one thousand, thousand legacies.

Parenthetical to the stream of consciousness of which we benefit today, the cavalcade of original thinkers created form without conformity; we are humbled when we think of them: Homer, Sophocles, Hippocrates, Plato, Pythagoras, Euclid, Galileo, Copernicus and thousands of others whose progressive genius seems to have culminated in Newton and Tesla. Within the context of time, our thoughts and theirs are parenthetical to the future. So it is, indeed, with humility that we present our ideas because they are only a remarkably small segment of a continuum. We are humbly thankful for this foundation which those before us created and from which we are so fortunate to advance: breadth of concept, curvilinear brilliance, extravagantly rich fields in which to conduct research and their clarion affects upon our excavation into the psyche. The works of Adler, Maslow, Jung, Freud and many others are indispensable in this case. So we should be humble as we consider all the talent that has gone before us—all the talent that lights our way.

Time Transcendence

As if in a dream, where happenings fly past in
ephemeral and multicolored precipitancy, the
experience of performing our talents exudes
timelessness from the depths of our subconscious.
Like the fascination of the ever-changing glimmer
within a multicrystaline prism, our talent welcomes
us to a wealth of life-fascination. Those of us
discovering such a sparkling prism, *how to best use
ourselves,* experience time-warp. If you experience
being lost in the present, you will want to return to
this state again and again. Its value is apparent when
seeing others who are bored with life itself. And, to be
sure, boredom is the condition of the disingenuous
self fraught with an ambiguity to use or to not use
talent. But being lost in the present while using our
talent is the precise opposite—the experiential
condition of purpose.

When Nicola Tesla would conduct experiments for
days without stopping for food or water, it seemed
only a few hours to him. Many times I have used my
talents from early afternoon to daybreak, for over
fourteen hours without realizing the transition of time
'til I heard birds welcoming the new day with their
songs, surprised to see that morning had come. Yet, it

seemed like the gentle passing of a pleasant dream.

During work, why does the transpiring of time accelerate for some and slow down for others? Why does the past and future become irrelevant, virtually nonexistent except as we need its positive use? Why do the concerns of the past and the uncertainty of the future fade as the clarity of the present brightens its aura surrounding us? What is this psyche connection with Eternity which superimposes itself over the monotony of time?

Relativism, the theory that truths originate from individual, spatial perspectives and, therefore, varies, is an explanation of time's elasticity. As in the case of psychosynthesis and the psychological elegance of talent, this time warp is accentuated with the equipoise of our knowledge and sub-knowledge which is best attained by the exigent expansion of talent; this mental balance allows concentration of supreme intensity for which time seems oblivious.

It is fatuously apparent that we cannot use our talents at all times, yet, because of the overarching and therefore holistic effect of psychosynthesis, we can live within its influence; the performance of our talent, however, is still the psychological crescendo for it sets the tone and tint of our lives. Within the world of our mind, within the world of cerebral mechanics, talents's omnipotence is complete; its momentary use, over time, can emancipate the life-wish, reordering a new world of the psyche for a lifetime. This momentary use, this genesis, this psychologic moment can occur in a millisecond when a molecular collision within the neuroglia causes a psychogenic awakening, a very real suspension beyond the metaphysical gravity of the human condition, concentrating while simultaneously expanding life. Thus, the time warp.

And although talent requires a lifetime of work and is beautifully never complete, it is time transcending work of the most sublime. That's why Austrian intellectual Stefan Sweig said, "A human being is not fully alive except when his best energies are at work; and when feeling is active, time moves swiftly though the clock-hands circle at their customary pace. Then, as in dreams one under the stress of powerful effects lives through measureless epochs between two ticks of the pendulum, and with each of us it is as with the enchanted man in the folktale who fancied that he spent a thousand years in the interval between two heartbeats."

Triumph, Fun and Concentration

Don't even need to try,
not to really, really fly,
it just happens when I go there.

Ever-changing, many-sided mobile,
variegated, kaleidoscopic Sundial,
just happens when you go there.

Ten billion laughing Suns,
ten billion laughing ones,
just happen when we go there.

Quasi-purple jasmine music,
wakes us laughing as we use it,
greets us every time we come here.

Flying in fluorescent dreams,
effervescent silver streams,
just happens as we smile here.

There exist no better way to experience triumph than
self-abandonment, the lifestyle of those who
consistently use their talent with all their hearts. To be
sure, pleasant amusement is an important part, a
necessary part of their job description. For as we use

our talents, even within the serious creative process, we have joyful recreation which may intensely, seamlessly last for many days. Nicola Tesla, unquestionably the world's greatest inventor, chose the word "rapture" to describe the experience of using his talent. Rapture is an interesting state. Of course, Tesla was at the height of inventiveness while experiencing it. He was at play. Yet, his power was controlled. On the other hand, there are the necros at play—wild "epilepsies" of maniacal enthusiasms. And then there is the vita at play—orchestrating every life-memory under the "conductorship" of talent, transcending the past and future to, with psychic and psyche, unconditionally absorb the present. This dynamic of the vita, of course, is why normal children concentrate for hours, consumed with unbridled innocent lust for the sparkling fascination in which they gleefully rhapsodize. And we, as adults, should never, never stop playing in this way. We should not behave exactly as children, only similarly, for our excitation should be inspired by the unobstructed absorption of the present, the adult form of play during the complete use of our talent. And this brings us to one of the most compelling problems of reconciling the dichotomy of labor and talent: concentration.

Ideally, the attractiveness and fascination of our work should absorb our emotional and mental powers so that concentration is flowing and natural without a forced feeling that might be verbalized as, "I am required to do this and must make myself do it." Neurotically commanding ourselves to do the things we dislike can never produce excellence. This strenuous, compulsive effort is but a similitude of concentration but not the one we experience while using our talents. Dr Frederick S. Perls describes the type of concentration which we should desire—the type closely associated with our childlikeness:

"Watch children at their games and you will see that they are concentrating on what they are doing to such a degree that it is difficult to draw their attention away. You will note also that they are excited about what they are doing. These two factors—attention to the object or activity and the excitement of satisfying need, interest or desire through what one is attentive to—are the substance of healthy concentration."

Likewise, talent is experienced with a spontaneous concentration which may seem inexhaustible to those who pursue excellence; this spontaneous concentration, found uniquely in the use of our talents, is measureless, Eternal. It is my theory that this childlike abandonment to talent unites the fore-conscious and aft-conscious as nothing else can; it is the unique reconciliation of our childlikeness with our adultness. For only when we are at play are we completely human and completely our original self. Talent, therefore, is the ultimate game.

This is a meta-conscious state in which no effort to concentrate is needed. Actors and actresses experience meta-consciousness when they are swept up and lost in a character. A stunning example is the performance in the film, *Camelot*. Some people feel this may be the finest acting ever portrayed in cinematography. Paradoxically, the stars of that film, Richard Harris, Vanessa Redgrave and Franco Nero, did not act. They, instead, lived their roles. They *were* King Arthur, Guenevere and Sir Lancelot—living these parts, losing themselves unto their characters. In the Alfred Hitchcock masterpiece, *Suspicion*, Cary Grant did not play the part of presumptuous charmer, Johnnie Aysgarth. Cary Grant—with a stellar array of nuance and subtlety—*was* Johnnie Aysgarth.

Another example of meta-consciousness is an artist who was commissioned by a company to create an Art Deco masterpiece. He said, "Before I could really begin to enjoy it, it was finished. The feeling registered that I was finished. It was complete. It was as though the image came to me subliminally." I have seen this piece of art and it possesses sublime, rhythmical movements and poetic symmetries that are stunning. He was obviously in a meta-conscious state when creating it.

Athletes who are lost in the instant of play are often described as *playing out of mind* or *playing in the zone*. This is the meta-conscious state in which athletes triumph. Yet, the desire to win can be so intense that the conscious mind becomes usurper. With analyses, critic and harsh judgment, the conscious begins shouting instructions to the player. Imagine a teacher shouting instructions of how to play to children at recess. The children would almost certainly stop playing. This is merely because it is the subconscious that plays, not the conscious. That is why golf great Bobby Jones said, "If I have two swing thoughts, I have no chance at all. If I have one, maybe I'll have a good shot. If I have none, *then* I can play like Bobby Jones." Thinking about the correct way to swing a golf club, a tennis racquet or pass a football is not fun because *thinking* about how to play is not playing. It is no surprise then, when athletes stop having fun they sometimes start losing. They have essentially stopped playing for the same reason children stop playing when they are no longer having fun. Perhaps they are no longer having fun because a teacher, like the conscious mind, is malevolently shouting instructions about how she wants them to play. Adults or children can never have fun in this way.

The dilemma of fantastic desire to win becoming conscious determination without subconscious fluidity leads to "choking." This is quite easy to discuss with aplomb from the comfort and safety of the sidelines. Nonetheless, digressing from a winning streak to choking is merely the conscious mentality becoming dominant. For, the athlete wants to win and knows how to do so but does not consciously possess the singular ability. This ability is only found within the equipoise of the vita-empowered mind. Above all, the game must contain an element of fun in order for the subconscious to make the ultimate performance. This is why Joe Montana, thought to be one of the greatest football players of all time, would make lighthearted remarks while preparing for the most competitive moments of an important game.

Thus, we consciously learn to act. We consciously learn to create art or play a game. But it is the subconscious which becomes the undisguised, unconcocted character, christens oil and canvass a living thing or crowns athletes with that laureled wreath of triumph.

Midst all the profundity, however, our talent must be fun. For, the experience of fun while working at our talent means something is wonderfully right. Fun in general is more than laughter between friends playing beach ball on a balmy tropical shore, more than frolic between lovers, more than the exuberant release of multiple emotions while dancing, more than uproarious laughter with friends. It is all these things and more. It is triumph. We laugh and experience joy as we do all these things because these are acts of triumph. We triumph over the cosmological gravity, the down-drag, the defiant giants which besiege mankind causing its loss of animated love. We triumph as we overpower any condition which imposes a lackluster veil of boredom upon us. Yet, undoubtedly, fun is not the absence of problems. If it were, no one would have fun. That is why Henry Beecher said, "Man without mirth is like a wagon without springs in which one is caused disagreeably to jolt at every pebble." If we allow ourselves to receive a "jolt at every pebble," we certainly can't be triumphant; and, we will clearly run across many pebbles and, indeed, many giant boulders on our journey to talent.

It is clarifying to note that triumph is experienced quite differently among personality temperaments. For our illustrative purposes, we need only consider two of the four personality types which Hippocrates discovered: the melancholy (maestro, mathematically and musically inclined, shy, sensitive, quiet, faithful, honest) and the sanguine (extremely social, people-oriented, outspoken, sometimes unreliable, possessing a high threshold of enjoyment).

For those, like Sir Isaac Newton, who are predisposed to a melancholy approach to their talent, triumphant fun may be experienced in outward silence and solitude. But within the mind of such a melancholy temperament there exists a vast world of artistry of which ordinary men have not dreamt. Tesla was also predisposed to this melancholic inwardness wherein which many detailed, technical statistics were analyzed and experiments conducted that lasted for days all achieved by his memory whereas his peers required a full laboratory and staff to assist them; yet, even then, they could never begin to approach his genius.

For those who are more sanguine, lighthearted

playfulness is one of the best indicators that we have found our primary element; the depth of fun while performing our talent, in turn, indicates our talent's depth and visa-versa. Observe the performance of a proven master to see their fullest animation. The tone of Sir Paul McCartney's on stage performance is one of cheeriness, a sort of victoriousness over all things dull. Away from the stage, when he is alone writing songs, using his talent is still more like fun than work. He says, "Every time I come to write a song, there's this magic little thing where I go, 'Ooh, ooh, it's happening again.' I just sort of sit down at the piano and go, 'I don't know this one.' And suddenly there's a song."

It is true that we want to take our talents seriously; yet, at the same time, they should be pleasantly diverting, as it evidently is for Sir Paul. For talent is not a thing we force upon ourselves but one which we are magnetized toward. Fluidity denotes relaxation and it is this coolness which we want to emulate in the expression of our true self. This is the opposite of aloofness or arrogance which, as we have discovered, dulls our sensitivity to the subconscious, the source of all creativity. For, to be certain, stuffiness is merely a shroud of insecurity diluting the interpretation of our subconscious life-events. That's why Charles Montesquieu said, "Great lords have their pleasures, but the people have fun." The most lasting, genuine fun is the expression of flinging wide the floodgates of the wonder world wherein which creativity and triumph reciprocate with one another upon the most brilliant coordinates of artistry. Whether expressed in a melancholy or sanguine temperament, talent is fun; and, fun is an emotional necessity. "Superfluous is a very necessary thing," said Voltaire.

Precocity

Ubiquitous novelty experienced when a child mixed with an infantile closeness to our subconscious may automatically draw us to our talent.

Did you love to draw when a child? Did you love to speak before your class, write, solve arithmetic problems or play an instrument? This is something which should be recalled by anyone wishing to discover their special skill. It is likely the thing you loved to do as a child is the very thing with which you are most gifted as an adult.

I recall a fellow student who I always felt was no ordinary human being. He was extremely refined and well mannered which are often signs of high intellect. My perceptions proved to be correct.

At the age of twelve he attained a certain virtuosity as a pianist creating sublime melodies to which his contemporaries seemed oblivious. He gave a concert for us, his classmates, and we ascribed to him the awe of celebrity.

His acclaim spread to New York and Los Angeles. Then he played before a live televison audience of more than twenty million people. He won a scholarship to the Juilliard School of Music. His precocity was abundantly apparent to all—to all save his parents.

They insisted that he become an accountant. He acquiesced and acquired a certain amount of success providing a nice lifestyle for a wife and children. But he missed his mistress. When missing her with particular longing, he would drink a little to ease the heartache. This worked for a while. But the law of diminishing returns demanded more drink to compensate for the greater pain. He eventually became an alcoholic and lost everything.

Then he returned to his first love; for the love of Mistress Talent is, for many people, incomparable. That's why Picasso said, "A man's work is his real seduction."

We often find this virtuous mistress at a young age.

Non-Materialism, Reciprocity and Self-Concept

Another phenomenon of psychologic elegance which compliments dynamic talent is the independence of materialism. This is primarily the case because using one's talent is emotionally reciprocal. It gives back. The only experiences equally reciprocal in this sense is the love of a paramour (presumably a spouse) one's children, dear friends or, perhaps, a dog. Talent's reciprocation is viscerally gratifying making it unnecessary to seek the satisfaction of the nonliving such as money and the inanimate things it buys. Should money be the predominate objective of using our talent, although it may appear that we have attained state-of-the-art, we will impose subliminal limitations upon our virtuosity. As Rudyard Kipling said, ". . . and no one shall work for money, and no one shall work for fame, but each for the joy of working . . ."

To understand more fully the immense value of talent's reciprocation let us consider it by comparative antithesis: watching television is an example of emotional non-reciprocity. When watching televison, one gives living vision, hearing and thought to a nonliving object. In this relationship with the nonliving, some often choose to compensate by eating for eating is a physically, emotionally gratifying experience whereas watching televison is not. Indeed, some find it impossible to watch television without eating although they are not in the slightest need of nourishment or even hungry. It is also interesting to note that since the advent of multi-channel televison, obesity has become pandemic. Perhaps this is symptomatic of a neurotic yearning for gratification rather than a yearning to be entertained or for a distraction from the pressing matters of the day. Indeed, in many cases both watching television and overeating appear to be a compensations and facsimiles for genuine validation.

In contradistinction, talent's reciprocation is powerfully unique. Rather than being based upon our relationship with family and friends—relationships that can be quite fickle—or with inanimate objects or food, it is based upon a loving relationship with ourselves which is faithfully dependable and, ironically, unselfish. *Talent, therefore, may be the very quintessence of self-love.*

This reciprocal phenomenon of talent is, therefore, quite possibly the most intelligent way to improve our self-esteem. But then, what is self-esteem? I define it this way:

It is the belief that we can be successful at work and that we are worthy of love.

I feel that using one's talent is indispensable to realize this belief about oneself. Not only is our relationship with others predetermined by our self-concept, it is also a universal determinate of our success, nonsuccess, fulfillment and disappointment, whom we marry, the friendships we make, the amount of money we earn and the extent to which we use our talent. All are underpinned by our self-estimation. Again, I feel there exists no greater balm which heals and sustains our self-concept than the use of our talent. For, as we have learned, talent takes all our life episodes and orchestrates them unto a symphony equating value. Its projected value being materialized as painting, poem or pantheon. Yet, before painting poem or pantheon is materialized, it must be derived from a value intrinsic—our original self which we highly esteem. We regard our self with this high estimation because we recognize *it is working as it* wishes. Thus it is functioning super-laboriously and thus it is producing by manifesting our talent. Our worthiness of love, it seems, is then more easily countenanced.

Honesty

Now let's think about two types of honesty as it relates to our talent: first, we will consider if we possess artistic talent or technical talent; secondly, we will consider personal integrity and how it may affect our talent.

Artists awaken upon the morning, the grandiose daybreak when the distinction is made between the *how* and *why* of one's talent. As Aristotle said in *Metaphysics*, those who understand *how* are mechanics while those who understand *why* are philosophers of their talent and may, therefore, be referred to as artists. In this sense an artist may certainly be a mechanic, but some mechanics can never be artists.

Those who understand the philosophical order of their talent probably possess some ability to teach others the nuances and subtleties of their respective craft. But those who are purely technical are lacking in the ability to teach an art for they do not comprehend the understanding of those same nuances and subtleties. It seems that Nicolas Poussin, a French painter who lived during the Seventeenth Century, is a superb example of a technical-philosopher for he prescribed a scientific methodology of art and beauty. Indeed, Poussin was the first, of whom we are aware, to philosophize a science of artistic beauty created by ceratin shapes and colors and their combinations.

Now, on the other hand, after some rehearsal, a mechanic could teach such an artistic idea from memory or from a textbook. Yet, a mechanic could never teach such ideas with authenticity for he could never conceive and then create such original ideas.

It is important to note that individuals who comprise a representative sample of any society could be recruited for an oil painting class and an artist with the talent of Nicolas Poussin himself could be recruited as the instructor. The class could study and experiment for years. But unless at least one of those recruited students happened to be an artist, all of that sublime teaching would have been wasted. The point is simple. Artistry of any kind cannot be imparted through education to those who are not artists. Technique can be imparted, but artistic philosophy cannot. I have witnessed this fact time after time while a student in several art classes.

This is why some people feel that healthy boundaries should be resumed between vocational-technical training, university training and art schools. For example, a large, major state university graduated one of their students bestowing upon him the degree of Bachelor of Arts although he was totally illiterate. Why was he even allowed to pass from the second grade without the ability to read one simple sentence? In another example, I edited a book for a man who "earned" a Doctorate in Education from an internationally known private university. His first and only language was English. After my editing was complete, I discovered during a conversation with him that he had never heard of the *Odyssey* or of Mark Twain. How can anyone, whose first and only language is English, complete grammar school, junior high school, high school, a bachelor's program, a master's program and a doctorate program in education yet only posses the ability to write at a high school level and be utterly oblivious to the *Odyssey* and Mark Twain?

Apparently, neither of these two gentlemen were artists yet they were granted degrees by well-known universities designating them as artist in orthodox terms and in the terms ascribed by Aristotle. If we presume they were mechanically-minded in the technical sense, rather than artists, they would, nonetheless, possess talent that is utterly indispensable to society; in these cases, their unique technical skill could have been overlooked. Thus, it is important to acknowledge whether our talent is artistic or mechanical or a hybrid of both and to pursue it accordingly.

Now we will consider honesty as it relates to our talent within the connotation of practical, day-to-day integrity:

Unfettered talent is the climax of civilization. For talent refined by disciplined *honesty* is self-redemption; and, only by honestly redeeming oneself, may society be redeemed. This is the kiss of life to the individual. This is the kiss of life to society. Even a few individuals who exercise their talents with disciplined honesty can redeem millions of others. Think of all that Sir Isaac Newton bequeathed to mankind through his disciplined study of celestial mechanics and calculus and its foray into scientific research of all kinds. Some historians, such as Michael Hart, feel that his selfless, quiet life directly influenced the world more than any other secular person in history.

This honesty we seek allows the simultaneous release of many suppressed life episodes during the act of self-truthfulness expertly formulated in our talent.

On the other hand, outside the boundaries of honesty, our ability to use our talent to the uttermost will be impossible since an ulterior motive exists within our mind and, consequently, the weakened vita will be neutralized by necros. So, rather than one motive, the singularity of which empowers us with direction, the necros introduce other motives until the vita has been diluted at which time our talent, no longer formulating the vita, also assumes a directionless nature.

It brings me no joy at all to say that the illiterate man who was given an unearned Bachelor's Degree is in prison and the man who was given an unearned Bachelor's Degree, Master's Degree and Doctorate is involved in a questionable profession.

A Compelling Reason:

Now that we have found our first love, how then shall we keep her?

We shall seek that benefactress *Passionate Belief.* For, above all, it is paramount that we have a passionate, compelling reason to use our talent in which we believe. This reason must be a healthy compulsion. It must be a reason bigger than ourselves which is wholly unattainable yet which, time and again, completely gratifies the full essence of our personhood; yes, it must be an all-compelling reason which, upon its completion, is joyfully renewed satisfying a taste subtly refined by the idiosyncratic backdrop of our life and, therefore, perpetuating the endless novelty of our talent.

There may be many times when we are tempted to surrender. But always remember this: *the perfect antidote for unbelief is the sheer experience of talent.*

Such was the immensity of Edwin Hubble's unique gift. Considered to be the greatest astronomer since Galileo, he discovered that other galaxies exist beyond our Milky Way and that the Universe, contrary to Albert Einstein's theories, is expanding with inconceivable speed. He said, "Labor, which is labor and nothing else, becomes an aversion. Work, to be pleasant, must be toward some great end; an end so great that dreams of it, anticipation of it overcomes all aversion to labor. So, until one has an end which he identifies with his whole life, work is hardly satisfactory." His wife described him in this way: "There was a sense of power, channeled and directed in an adventure that had nothing to do with personal ambition. There was hard concentrated effort and yet detachment. The power was controlled."

But even Hubble had his challenges. Although we have found our talent, the journey is not easy. Yet, the greater our compelling reason to use our talent, the greater also will be the distance which we travel. Here, it may be best to illustrate these ideas with a story:

William wanted to go to the palisaded, crystal City of Talent of which he had heard so many wondrous tales. It seemed that social gravity subsided within the walls of this almost celestial city where everyone's talent was freely experienced causing an ambience of fulfilled wishes.

But there were giants.

They despised the city and all who wanted to enter therein. They lived along the path of the city and were obsessed with fully destroying the courage of anyone who set foot upon the path, forcing him back to the poverty-stricken City of Mediocrity. Nonetheless, William was determined. So he set out upon the path which, he soon discovered, was difficult to follow itself. To add to this discouragement, he met three others who were walking back toward the City of Mediocrity and, with much persuasion, tried to get him to turn back as well. But he went forward, although now he was fraught with doubts.

After traveling all day and into the night, he stopped for repose. His clean conscious, free of ambiguity since he was on the right road, permitted a deep sleep which was visited by visions of the beautiful city's splendor. Rustling awake upon the dawn, William felt the presence of someone in his company. Incredulous upon the sight of a defiant giant, William shuddered, his heart almost stopping. A huge man! He jumped to his feet and backed away at which retreat the giant assumed a posture of increased confidence. Seeing that he was in trouble and defenseless against this human beast, he cleverly did something the ogre had not seen before. He began to laugh.

It was a contrived, cocksure laugh. Yet it freed him to laugh again. And the more he laughed, the more the giant's posture and countenance began to droop. So William laughed louder and stepped forward with the assuredness of a general. Then reaching for a nearby rock, he hurled it at the giant as hard as he could. The giant roared with anger. So William picked up another, bigger stone and threw it harder, all the time stepping forward. The giant then ran away.

William raised his arms in triumph and, dancing a jig, victoriously cheered and laughed!

He rejoined his journey confident that the path leading to the City of Talent would be easy from here on.

That evening, just before twilight as he entered the Black Forest, he smelled a foul odor that he thought must have come from a dead animal. Or was it that odor from the giant he sent running? The smell became worse.

Then in the wooded path before him, narrowly framed on either side by the tall trees, stood that giant he thought he'd never see again. William turned to retreat a few paces and, behold, another giant guarded him from behind. Then, crushing trees as men push back barley from before them as they walk through a field, two more giants on either side of the path cleared timber with the sound of crashing thunder. The four giants glared down on him with hideous grins. William breathed deeply, which was a good start. He nervously placed his hands upon his hips assuming the posture of a mocker. Yet, his attempt to let out a laugh sounded artificial, his voice shaking with the kind of fear which paralyzes. William stood frozen still. There was torturing silence.

Suddenly the giant that William had chased away earlier that very morning picked him up by the leg and threw him to the ground with such ferocity that he thought to himself as he lay there, "Surely my soul is departing." Then all the ogres took turns treating him shamefully, beating him and leaving him for dead. He could barely move, neither could he sleep nor find any comfort for ten of the longest of his days.

But not being among those who surrender, since his cause was so great, he went forward. Sometimes his gate was more like falling forward then walking. But he kept moving.

He encountered more giants. Yet, as long as he laughed at them and began immediately to hurl stones at them, he found he could chase them all away.

These tests of his courage and his long, difficult journey lasted many years. But along the way, the evidence that he was on the correct path increased because the enthralling beauty of the area increased with each step until he finally reached the gates of the city to which he was warmly welcomed. And William lived happily ever after, most of the time, in the City of Talent.

Like William's willpower, vita-empowered-talent is continually primed with magnificent drive which draws some people forward, ever forward to the pinnacle of expertise. Courage is required to accept a challenge on so grand a scale that we are awed by its endlessness.

Nicolas Tesla was a living example of the vita-empowered-talent. He said, "When a child I asked 'What is electricity?' and found no answer. Eighty years have gone by, and I am still unable to answer it." This perennial fascination of electricity was one of the compelling reasons he used his talent of scientific invention without reservation. Yet his primary compelling reason was to "provide free electricity to the world." This gave him phenomenal willpower for his research of electricity, at times concentrating uninterrupted for long periods without food or water superceding the laws of human energy.

Lord Kelvin, an English scientists said, "Tesla has contributed more to electrical science than any other man." Many people feel, as I do, that he also eclipsed Thomas Edison's inventiveness. In fact, Edison failed to honor a contract with Tesla on two occasions, refusing to pay large sums of money he legally owed him. Edison even tried to ruin Tesla's inventions because of their complete superiority to his. Yet, because Tesla's reason for using his talent was truly compelling, he focused upon it rather than Edison's negative energy, and so he never gave up. Later, in 1890, George Westinghouse gave Tesla a check for one million dollars, a fantastic fortune at that time, along with a contract for many more millions. These contracts made Tesla so remarkably wealthy that George Westinghouse and the huge Westinghouse Corporation would have collapsed if Tesla sold his stock. So, in an August act of benevolence, Tesla tore his stock certificates in pieces and handed them to Westinghouse.

One of Tesla's most influential inventions was a complete abstraction and a *total* impossibility to the world's most advanced electrophysicists. Yet, every modern home, every place of business or commercial enterprise around the world uses it to conduct electricity. That single invention, polyphase alternating currents, which we refer to as A/C, has revolutionized the world. He also began the science of robotics. He invented solar power. He invented X-rays, the same ones used by every doctor throughout the international medical community. It is unpleasant to imagine what the world would be like without X-rays. He invented devices which would create controlled electrical storms, directing their power for the use of mankind. Astonishingly, Tesla invented a global internet, a worldwide communication network which would allow anyone in the world, no matter where they were located, to talk to each other and hear radio broadcasts all on a device the size of a wrist watch. Yet, his worldwide network was far more sophisticated than ours: first, it was not dependent upon telephone wires or fiber optics but an infrastructure of super-concentrated radio waves and, secondly, its use was to be free of charge for all mankind. Then he invented another device that completely changed our world as much as polyphase alternating currents; Tesla invented radio communications of all kinds including remote control. Radio waves are, of course, the premise for television. Guglielmo Marconi received world acclaim for the invention of the radio because he demonstrated it first in public; yet his demonstration revealed that he relied heavily upon Tesla's research. It was clearly documented that Tesla invented the radio first.

Tesla, however, was humble without the slightest trace of material ambition or desire for fame—a man who seemingly personified the oriental maxim, "It is the glory of a man to overlook an offense." He did not retaliate for Marconi's usurpation but, maintaining princely dignity, went forward guided by his compelling reason to use his talent and simply ignored Marconi. "Let him continue," Tesla said, "he's using seventeen of my [radio] patents."

Later in his life Tesla said, "Speaking for myself, I have already had more than my measure of this exquisite enjoyment, so much that for many years my life was little short of continuous rapture." Why did he feel this way? Although he was ruthlessly cheated by selfish, greedy men and overshadowed by egomaniacs who stole his inventions, why did he never think of giving up? The answer is this: he possessed a specific, compelling reason to use his talent. Talent was the thing that empowered his ability to believe. Then, in turn, didn't his belief empower his talent? Yes, like a double helix spiraling ever upward, one empowering the other, they are compliments in rhapsody.

One morning just after daybreak, I recall seeing two hawks spiral through the air with a stunning elaboration of acrobatics. How high, how swift, how daring! I marveled before their lightening majesty, their breathtaking feats of ariel poetry for almost one hour. They were unmistakably aware of my presence for they would return over and again to the small tree I sat beneath. How could they miss me with their penetrating eyes? They were proud of their sky ruling abilities before me, a common Earth-bound man. What love they had for one another and for me, as well. Yet, if only one of them had been there on that blissful dawn, the skyward stage would have been dark, so to speak, and their theater of the bright heavens missed. They rejoiced *together* with the innocent love of two mates, as do talent and passionate belief.

Now, in benediction to our journey, let's consider another illustration of talent and passionate belief:

It was like a dream of desperately needing to run but being enveloped in ethereal gravity rendering slow, arduous movement of his arms and legs as though laden with the heaviest lead. It was so much like a dream. Fraught with jerking and imbalance, his fight to run advanced a few feet and stopped where, leaning on his two canes, he solemnly looked at his trembling legs, then toward his friends. Without thinking, the others had dashed before him and their agility was exquisite cruelty. How wrong was their strength—how wrong was their ability to run like normal, healthy young men. Now they were all aboard, laughing, jostling one another about having just made it before the train pulled out of the station. Then they saw him through the carriage window and, for a half-second, froze, trying to take in the sight of his battle of the heart. His friend, Carter, leapt from his seat and, with one of the others, sprinted to him then half carried him onto the train as it moved down the tracks toward London. His four friends gratuitously laughed so their deep concern would be hidden but he left the presence of the group, as it were, silently gazing out the window, remembering.

Was I really on the rowing team at Oxford? Was it really in this world that, with inspiration of a few beers and my friends, I climbed the foot bridge at Oxford and in bold letters painted "vote liberal" across its side? Did I do that? Did I move about with moxie in the inner circle of the elite bearing an attitude of unyielding confidence? Was it with the same body that I walked, ran or stood so effortlessly and expressed myself in a thousand subtle ways with perfect equilibrium? Why this waste of my energy and dignity which was formerly manifested in sophisticated aplomb? Why must I now endure *this*?

He remembered the past New Years Eve party when most of the wine he had tried to pour into a glass flooded the tablecloth and, politely, none of his friends mentioned it although this little accident created a mutual foreboding among them; the night of mixed blessings; the night he knew his health had begun to worsen; the night he began to fall in love with Jane Wilde. He thought of the series of tests he had undergone while in hospital and the way in which the doctors reacted.

"After all that they didn't tell me what I had, except that it was not multiple sclerosis, and that I was an a-typical case. I gathered, however, that they expected it to continue to get worse, and that there was nothing they could do, except give me vitamins. I could see that they didn't expect them to have much effect. I didn't like asking for more details, because they were obviously bad. The realization that I had an incurable disease that was likely to kill me in a few years, was a bit of a shock. How could something like that happen to me? Why should I be cut off like this?"

The doctors had warned him that, although he was only twenty-one, his time could be short—so short that he may be unable to complete his PhD. With the specter of death hovering over him like a dark cloud he despaired of life and withdrew from others seeking temporary comfort in large doses of wine while listening to Wagner. But Jane Wilde was there and became a significant source of his recovery from depression, boosting his ability to believe in his talent.

". . . while I had been in hospital, I had seen a boy I vaguely knew die of leukemia in the bed opposite me. It had not been a pretty sight. Clearly there were people who were worse off than me. At least my condition didn't make me feel sick. Whenever I feel inclined to feel sorry for myself I remember that boy. Before my condition had been diagnosed, I had been very bored with life. There had not seemed anything worth doing. But shortly after I came out of hospital, I dreamt that I was going to be executed. I suddenly realized that there were a lot of worthwhile things I could do if I were reprieved. Another dream, that I had several times, was that I would sacrifice my life to save others. After all, if I were going to die anyway, it might as well do some good. But I didn't die."

With remarkable bravery, he began to transform this disaster into an opportunity; he awakened to his feelings about life and the most bold path upon which to take his talent. He didn't choose small objectives. Rather, he became fascinated with the dichotomy of the prevailing theory of gravity and quantum mechanics—a fascination which would propel his talent further and further to the pinnacle of cosmological science: discovering the overarching equation which ubiquitously corresponds to everything in the Universe. Ironically, his body could continue to waste away without the slightest detriment to his talent for he was pursuing a PhD in Theoretical Physics at Cambridge and his mind was the only tool he would ever truly need. Indeed, his ability to create theoretical methodologies of Byzantine intricacy was completely unaffected; so, as his body withered, his talent of intuitively solving extremely complex physics problems flourished.

It was a *tour de force* as he rushed to finish the research for his PhD. On many occasions, because he was losing the ability to walk, he arrived at the research center with bandages on his head having fallen heavily the day before. Always reluctant to endorse his debilitation, he was, however, soon forced to acquiesce to the aid of wheel chair. The loss of the ability to walk was a heartbreaking reality to accept; and this pain was deepened further by the deterioration of his speech which was becoming more and more slurred and rapidly became unintelligible.

Was he demoralized and despondent? Yes. Was he tempted to retreat? Yes. Did he bitterly cry? Yes, many times.

Why was he able to drag himself out of bed every morning into a wheel chair and continue his research? Why was he able to believe that he had a place in the world—a significant place? Why did others attribute tremendous value to him rather than pity? What emboldened his will to live, his determination to reconcile the contradiction of the prevailing theories of relativity? Why did he believe that he could find a new cosmological matrix which would solve the riddle of the Universe?

He was doing something that gave him an increased ability to believe. Day by day, with ever increasing confidence he began to develop his talent. That's why he said, "I think I'm happier now than before I started. Before the illness set in, I was very bored with life. I drank a fair amount. I guess I didn't do any work. It was really a rather pointless existence."

He discovered that using his talent was like playing when he was a child; and, just like a child, he never really became tired or bored with playing.

In spite of his troubles, things were looking up and his research, from strength to strength, gained international acclaim. He worked for many years. But the work was joyful to him. After all, it was his talent. Having made a number of momentous breakthroughs, he was given the Lucian Professorship at Cambridge, a position first held by Sir Isaac Newton. Then he received the greatest honor of his life. He was offered a membership in the Royal Society becoming the youngest member in its history. Next, he was made a Commander of the British Empire by Queen Elizabeth.

With Jane Wilde, now his wife, he attended numerous functions and socialized extensively. He had become a sought after celebrity and was invited to speak, with the aid of an interpreter, around the world.

While visiting Geneva Switzerland, he had intended to work on a book he was writing and conduct research when, in the middle of the night, he began to choke, gasping for air. Surely he could regain his breath. But he couldn't inhale. He panicked—he fought for breath. His body twitched and stiffened, writhing in his bed sheets.

Then clouds of blur.

He regained consciousness with a painful thud in his head and a horrible pain in his throat. A tracheotomy had been performed to save his life. Now it was impossible to utter a single intelligible word—his voice forever silenced.

Nevertheless, he quickly turned this tragedy into an opportunity; he had a speech synthesizer designed so he could now rapidly key-in words which would be reproduced phonetically and made audible by a speaker. Now everyone who spoke English could understand him perfectly.

After a period of recovery, he continued his research and speaking engagements then wrote a runaway best seller that jettisoned him to international stardom. He has been described as the toughest man alive with the most beautiful smile in the world.

He says, "I have had motor neuron disease for practically all my adult life. Yet, it has not prevented me from having a very attractive family, and being successful in my work. I have been lucky that my condition has progressed more slowly than is often the case. But it shows that one need not lose hope."

The use of his talent made him a passionate believer. For, indeed, the full use of his talent was the perfect antidote for his unbelief. So belief mixed with talent, that forceful ability to believe, is why people throughout the world associate the two words—genius and hero—with the name Stephen Hawking.

Concluding Thoughts

There is often a mysticism which shrouds the human wish for fulfillment. Many propose, many portend that we cannot be fulfilled in this life save for certain mystical prescriptions of transporting qualities. The life wish, however, is not as mysterious as some would have us believe. It is actually quite simple.

As Carl Jung said, "All neurosis is a substitute for legitimate suffering."

Likewise, *the unfulfilled wish* is a substitute for legitimate suffering.

The unfulfilled wish, then, is somewhat of a pretense. For we always posses the choice to suffer progressively or, in other words, suffer toward the state of fulfillment. We suffer unnecessarily within the state of nonfulfillment, paradoxically, because we want to avoid suffering. This is the impediment that the human race stumbles upon—the reluctance to suffer. In an infantile recalcitrance of our Earthly predicament, the figuratively poor, sick, uneducated, hungry malcontent rails against suffering and so insures his unhappiness. For mankind so often pretends suffering is a recompense for punishment; and we know from our childhood that all punishment, whether social or providential, is to be avoided.

Indeed, using one's talent is a glorious garden not without thorns. I just read about an actor who went for fifteen years without much work or money while he lived in what his doctor called "a state of shame." He had been wealthy and famous but now was broke. So, he was incorrectly ashamed of himself. We can empathically understand his feelings. He gave up relationships with paramours and humbly accepted his loneliness. A friend gave him money each week to help him keep going. But now he has been nominated for a prestigious award and there is talk that he may be nominated for an Oscar.

Was it worth it to continue to pursue his talent thereby opening his subconscious to a dialog upon its own terms? Was it worth it to suffer until the vita triumphed, unshackling the necros from their repressive states, freeing him from immobility, terminating an epoch of infancy or of adolescence which may have been waiting to be closed?

I know of an artist who never made one penny for his work. Like the actor, he spent fifteen years working at his talent. He painted for the sheer joy of creating while never seeking notoriety, giving himself to handcrafting his work. He was homeless a few times and bitterly embarrassed because of this. Now his work is coming to fluorescence. It is being praised and purchased.

Was it worth it to discover the most intelligent way in which to suffer, the recompense of which redeemed him unto himself and unto society?

Both men were single and had no children. If they had children, their first obligation would have been to provide a stable, nurturing home for them. For while survival and procreation are the two most important things, parenting, I feel, is third. There can be no better method of parenting than to *ever so gently* introduce a child to the idea of discovering his or her talent. To be sure, introducing one's children to their talent is the essence of parenting; for this is an act of teaching them to highly esteem themselves and, simultaneously, equipping them to work at the skill for which they are fully appropriate.

This is why, if we have been blessed with children, we must put them before our talent in order to provide a place of peace and safety for them. Of course, if we can provide peace and safety for our children while exercising our talent, then pursuit of talent is essential.

For then nothing under the Sun is more virtuous than that starry quest of our envisioned self we call talent. Talent! *Tutto a te mi guida!*—everything leads me to you!

Made in the USA